SPINNING SPIDERS

by Ruth Berman

photographs by
David T. Roberts and David M. Schleser

Lerner Publications Company • Minneapolis

This book is available in two editions:
Library binding by Lerner Publications Company, a division of Lerner Publishing
    Group, Inc.
Soft cover by First Avenue Editions, an imprint of Lerner Publishing Group, Inc.
241 First Avenue North
Minneapolis, MN 55401 U.S.A.

Website address: www.lernerbooks.com

Words in *italic* type are explained in a glossary on page 30.

Library of Congress Cataloging-in-Publication Data

Berman, Ruth.
    Spinning spiders / by Ruth Berman ; photographs
by David T. Roberts and David M. Shleser.
        p. cm. — (Pull ahead books)
    Includes index.
    Summary: Describes the physical characteristics
and behavior of spiders and how they use their silk for
weaving webs and other purposes.
    ISBN-13: 978-0-8225-3604-8 (lib. bdg. : alk. paper)
    ISBN-10: 0-8225-3604-8 (lib. bdg. : alk. paper)
    ISBN-13: 978-0-8225-3610-9 (pbk. : alk. paper)
    ISBN-10: 0-8225-3610-2 (pbk. : alk. paper)
    1. Spiders—Juvenile literature. 2. Spider webs—
Juvenile Literature. [1. Spiders.] I. Roberts, David T.,
ill. II. Schleser, David M., ill. III. Title. IV. Series.
QL458.4.B48   1998
595.4'4—dc21   98-3348

Manufactured in the United States of America
8 – PP – 9/1/11

What kind of animal is a spider?

Surprise! Spiders are not bugs or *insects*.

Spiders are *arachnids*.

An insect has three main
body parts and six legs,

but an arachnid has two main
body parts and eight legs.

Most spiders
have eight
eyes.

Some spiders have
two, four, or six eyes.
A few have no eyes!

How many
eyes does
this spider
have?

Spiders have small openings
at the back end of their body.

These openings are called *spinnerets*.

Strong, thin strings of silk come out of the spinnerets.

All spiders spin silk.

They use their legs to pull
and move the silk.

Spiders use their silk
in different ways.

Some
spiders
weave
webs like
this with
their silk.

Some webs are sticky traps.
Look! An insect is stuck in this web.

The spider
wraps
more silk
around it.

Then the spider eats the insect
by sucking out all its soft parts.

Some webs are spider homes.

This grass spider lives in a web shaped like a *funnel*.

Webs can be many shapes and sizes.

Spiders called *orb weavers* make round webs.

Some orb weavers spin zigzags
in their webs.

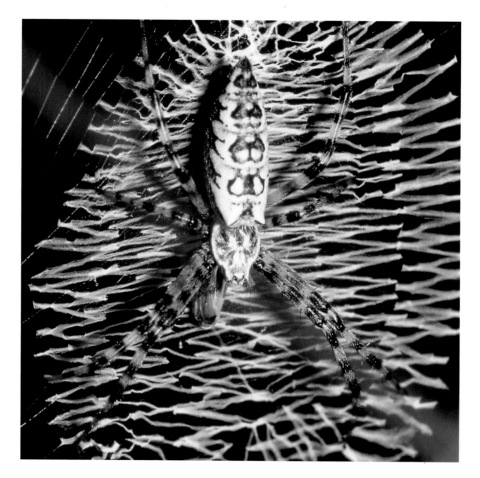

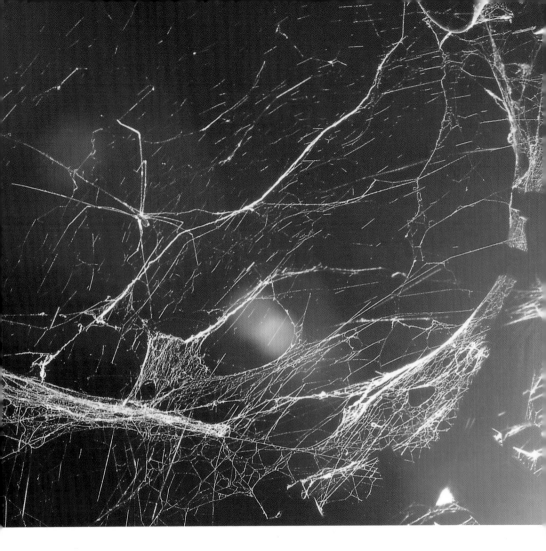

Other spiders spin messy webs.

Some spiders do not weave webs.

They use their silk in other ways.
Do you know how?

This spider lives in a *burrow.*
Its burrow is a long hole
in the ground.

The spider uses silk to make its
burrow soft and cozy.

Most female spiders spin silk around their eggs to make *egg sacs*.

Egg sacs protect the eggs.

Some spiders carry their egg sacs everywhere.

This spider is guarding her egg sac.

Can you guess how many eggs
are in this egg sac?

Baby spiders hatch from the eggs.

Baby spiders are called *spiderlings*.

Can you find the spiderlings here?

They are riding on their
mother's back!

Spiders use their silk in many ways.

Next time you see a spider, watch what it spins!

KEY:

shows where spiders live

Find your state or province on this map.
Do spinning spiders live near you?

Parts of a Spider's Body

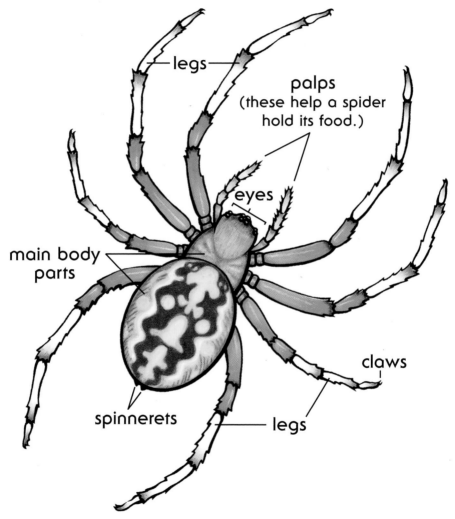

legs

palps
(these help a spider
hold its food.)

eyes

main body
parts

claws

spinnerets

legs

Glossary

arachnids: animals that have two body parts and eight legs

burrow: a long hole in the ground that some spiders use as their home

egg sacs: silk bags that female spiders spin around their eggs

funnel: a round, tunnel-like shape that is wide at one end and narrow at the other

insects: animals that have three body parts and six legs

orb weavers: spiders that spin round webs

spiderlings: baby spiders

spinnerets: openings at the back end of a spider's body where silk comes out

webs: nets of strong, thin strings of silk made by spiders

Hunt and Find

- spider **homes** on pages 14, 19
- spiders **catching** food on pages 12–13, 26
- **spiderlings** on pages 6, 24–25
- **egg sacs** on pages 20–23
- spiders **spinning** silk on pages 9–10
- spider **webs** on pages 3, 9, 11–17, 26

The publisher wishes to extend special thanks to our **series consultant,** Sharyn Fenwick. An elementary science-math specialist, Mrs. Fenwick was the recipient of the National Science Teachers Association 1991 Distinguished Teaching Award. In 1992, representing the state of Minnesota at the elementary level, she received the Presidential Award for Excellence in Math and Science Teaching.

About the Author

Ruth Berman was born in New York and grew up in Minnesota. As a child, she spent her time going to school and saving lost and hurt animals. Later, Ruth volunteered at three zoos and got her degree in English. She enjoys writing science books for children. Ruth lives in California with her husband Andy, her dog Hannah, and her two cats Nikki and Toby.

About the Photographers

In 1993 David and Deborah Roberts and David Schleser started Nature's Images, Inc., a natural-history writing and photography company. Their work has taken them to the rain forests and cloud forests of Costa Rica, Guatemala, and Hawaii, to the Amazon River regions of Peru and Brazil, and to the deserts of North and Central America. They research with many universities, museums, and government agencies. They also serve as expedition leaders for workshops in the Peruvian Amazon. Nature's Images is dedicated to helping people understand how fragile our world is.